A PUBLICATION TAXONOMY

AN INITIAL GUIDE TO ACADEMIC
PUBLISHING TYPES, INSIDE AND BEYOND
ACADEME

A Hybrid Publishing Consortium Production

Concept and editorial: Simon Worthington & Christina Kral
Thanks for feedback and contributions to: Gary Hall, Marcus Burkhardt and Pauline van Mourik Broekman

ISBN: 978-1-906496-70-8
Copyright © 2014 the authors
Creative Commons Attribution-ShareAlike 3.0 Germany
(CC BY-SA 3.0 DE)
http://creativecommons.org/licenses/by-sa/3.0/de/deed.en

Legend: This deed is used in the absence of an intellectual property framework that represents the authors respective position on copyright.

The Hybrid Publishing Consortium is a project of the Hybrid Publishing Lab in collaboration with partners and associates. The Hybrid Publishing Lab is part of the Leuphana University of Lüneburg Innovation Incubator, financed by the European Regional Development Fund and co-funded by the German federal state of Lower Saxony.

http://consortium.io
http://cdc.leuphana.com/structure/hybrid-publishing-lab/
http://hybridpublishing.org/

How to Participate and the Publishing Process

GitHub and WikiPedia

The taxonomy originates and is maintained on a GitHub repository under a Creative Commons ShareAlike licence. There is an open invitation for contributions to the list and the list item descriptions.

A Publication Taxonomy base URL
https://github.com/consortium/publication-taxonomy

The full list item descriptions can be found on WikiPedia and have been collected together as a WikiPedia community book.
https://en.wikipedia.org/wiki/Book:A_Publication_Taxonomy

You are welcome to add to the list of entries and to edit the articles on WikiPedia or on our GitHub repository if the WikiPedia bots or its requirement of a Neutral Point of View (NPOV) proves too infuriating and culturally shallow and you prefer a Critical Point of View (CPOV).

The issue and necessity of CPOV is outlined in the Institute of Network Cultures' publication from 2011, 'Critical Point of View: A Wikipedia Reader', available online, see
http://networkcultures.org/wpmu/cpov/

The Consortium and the Publishing Process

The collaborative list building project plays a role in the Consortium's research to understand how boundaries of publishing are shifting. The taxonomy will be used and published in a variety of forms, on an ongoing basis, with the Consortium team acting as list maintainers and editors.

CONTENTS

Introduction

Publication Taxonomy Summary

    Part 1
    Academic Publication and Document Types
    Part 2
    *Unconventional publications (Academic
    and Non-Academic), Hybrid and Experimental
    (Blue Sky)*

Publication Taxonomy Extended (descriptions)
    A synopsis of edited and appended WikiPedia entries

A full list can be found here
https://en.wikipedia.org/wiki/Book:A_Publication_Taxonomy

    Part 1
    Academic Publication and DocumentTypes
    Part 2
    *Unconventional Publications (Academic and
    Non-Academic), Hybrid and Experimental
    (Blue Sky)*

Publication Taxonomy Visual Appendix
    An image gallery of publication examples

Introduction

Dear Community,

Welcome to the Publication Taxonomy an exploratory listing project by the Hybrid Publishing Consortium.

The Hybrid Publishing Consortium is the technology research arm of the Hybrid Publishing Lab and is made up of a team of six interdisciplinary researchers, developing open source software for multi-format publishing. Creating an exploratory taxonomy of publication types plays a role in our software design process helping us understand the boundaries of publishing forms.

When the Consortium started to compile a list of the various types of scholarly publications we had to keep in mind the challenge of a continuously changing technology landscape. This meant moving to a so called post-digital condition (although a contested term)–involving parallel usage of various media types, a new collaborative paradigm, a proliferation of tool sets and open access academic publishing.

To give some limits around what we define as a publication we agreed on three very open parameters–(1) the act of making a document public, (2) the involvement of textuality, and (3) a scholarly/academic orientation.

Acceleration best describes the overall condition for both the development of publishing and the shaping of the emergent post-digital scholar, blurring the distinction between the publishers workflow and the scholars textual creation. The renegotiation of new roles for publisher and scholar is one area

Introduction

where new publishing types emerge, especially where the act of reading becomes a new textual creation. An instability arises in the scholarly workflow and how the scholar is organizing and adjusting her/his work steps within the post-digital condition. It also means an expansion of the very definition what constitutes a publication.

To add to the post-digital scholars' palette of opportunities we introduce dynamic publishing, an industry term to describe digital automated processes in publishing-distribution, rights management and reading analytics-to name a few areas.

Below you'll find a list compiled of various publication types that can currently be found on the publishing horizon. We tried to sort these established & emerging types and find a common definition for each. We did this to gain an overview of the forms available and the purposes they serve. We were and are looking at classic forms of publishing as well as hybrid forms, expanding to publications with enhanced options of interaction and engagement, investigating the potential of modularity, intermixing printed matter and digital media.

We came up with a list, parted into two sections:
PART 1 - conventional academic publications
PART 2 - unconventional, experimental types, appearing within and outside of academia.

The second part is to create a pool of possible directions for the publishing domain. As you can see this list not comprehensive. Therefore please feel invited to share your comments and types of publications you think relevant to include. For a better understanding of the options we'd greatly appreciate if you added an example, in form of a link or description.

You can direct your comments to Simon and Christina on our GitHub repository, via email or our @HyPub Twitter handle.

We thank you for your analytical readership.

Enjoy,
Simon and Christina – The Consortium, Hybrid Publishing Lab

Contact details:
simon.worthington@leuphana.de
christina.kral@leuphana.de
@HyPub
GitHub
https://github.com/consortium/publication-taxonomy

A Publication Taxonomy—an Initial Guide to Academic Publishing Types, Inside and Beyond Academe is a Hybrid Publishing Consortium initiative, as part of the Hybrid Publishing Lab, Centre for Digital Cultures in Lüneburg, Germany. The list will be hosted and updated on GitHub and published on our open research platform https://consortium.io/.

Publication Taxonomy Summary

PUBLICATION TAXONOMY SUMMARY

Part 1
ACADEMIC PUBLICATION AND DOCUMENT TYPES

- Academic book review
- Academic journal
—Special issue of an academic journal
—Data journal *(focus on interaction, reuse and traceable)*
—Overlay journal *(only online, compiled out of existing material, for reuse)*
—Published contribution to a discussion in a journal *(pre-print/post-print)*
- Anthology
- Conference poster
- Conference proceedings
- Course reader
- Edited book
- Edited collection
- Festschrift *(commemorative publication for an individual, "liber amicorum")*
- Educational pack
- Essay
- Gloss
- Graduate thesis
- Grey literature
- Minor or regional language publications
- Monograph
- Non-Western typographic book, *e.g., Chinese, Arabic, etc.*
- Published interviews
- Published reader
- PhD thesis
- Reading group
- Reading list
- Reference work
—Encyclopedia
—Compendium
—Handbook
—Manual
- Report
- Research paper, academic or scholarly paper
- Working paper

Part 2
UNCONVENTIONAL PUBLICATIONS (ACADEMIC AND NON-ACADEMIC), HYBRID AND EXPERIMENTAL (BLUE SKY)

- Apps
- Archive
- Artist's book
- Bibliography
- Blog
- Book review (Non-academic)
- Catalog
- Chat streams
- Conference proceedings (multimedia)
- Cookbook
- Discussion forums
- E-book
- Extremely compartmentalised information (security academia)
- Email
- Email list
- Exhibition zine
- Graphic (novel-type) book
- Guided tour
- Journal, science magazine, Magazine (academic and non-academic)
- Leak
- Lecture
- Lecture video
- Liquid book
- Map/geospatial representation
- Medium-length books *along the lines of Amazon's Kindle Singles*
- Multimedia book
- Nanopublishing
- Newspaper article
- Non-conventional journal
- Notebook, *e.g., Walter Benjamin's or Antonio Gramsci*
- Objects (digital/analogue)
- Open notebook
- Pamphlets, *e.g., The Atavist and Stanford Literary Lab*
- Podcasts
- Rapid SMS
- RSS feeds
- SMS
- Storify
- Ted Books
- Textbook
- Twitter (micro blog)
- Transmedia - distributed storytelling
- Video Documentation
- Video essay
- White paper
- Wikipedia page
- Wikis
- Zine

PUBLICATION TAXONOMY EXTENDED
A SYNOPSIS OF EDITED AND APPENDED WIKIPEDIA ENTRIES

A full list can be found here
https://en.wikipedia.org/wiki/Book:A_Publication_Taxonomy

You are welcome to add to the list of entries and to edit the articles on WikiPedia or on our GitHub repository if the WikiPedia bots or Neutral Point of View (NPOV) proves too infuriating and culturally shallow and you prefer a Critical Point of View (CPOV).

The necessity of CPOV is outlined in the Institute of Network Cultures' publication from 2011, 'Critical Point of View: A Wikipedia Reader', available online, see
http://networkcultures.org/wpmu/cpov/

Part 1
Academic Publication and Document Types

ACADEMIC BOOK REVIEW
Book reviews of scholarly books are checks upon the research books published by scholars; unlike articles, book reviews tend to be solicited. Journals typically have a separate book review editor determining which new books to review and by whom. If an outside scholar accepts the book review editor's request for a book review, he or she generally receives a free copy of the book from the journal in exchange for a timely review. Publishers send books to book review editors in the hope that their books will be reviewed. The length and depth of research book reviews varies much from journal to journal, as does the extent of textbook and trade book review. http://en.wikipedia.org/wiki/Academic_journal#Book_reviews

ACADEMIC JOURNAL
A peer-reviewed periodical in which scholarship relating to a particular academic discipline is published. Academic journals serve as forums for the introduction and presentation for scrutiny of new research, and the critique of existing research. Content typically takes the form of articles presenting original research, review articles, and book reviews.
http://en.wikipedia.org/wiki/Academic_journal

—Special issue of Academic Journal

—Data journal (focus on interaction and reuse, traceable)
peer reviewed data papers describing datasets with high reuse potential. Associated data is to be professionally archived, preserved, and openly available. Equally important, the data and the papers are citable, and reuse will be tracked.

In beta phase. http://openarchaeologydata.metajnl.com/about/ (+ changes)
—*Overlay journal (only online, compiled out of existing material, re-use)*
An overlay journal or overlay ejournal is a term for a specific type of open access academic journal, almost always an online electronic journal (ejournal). Such a journal does not produce its own content, but selects from texts that are already freely available online. While many overlay journals derive their content from preprint servers, others, such as the Lund Medical Faculty Monthly, contain mainly papers published by commercial publishers but with links to self archived pre- or post prints when possible.
The editors of such a journal locate suitable material from open access repositories and public domain sources, read it, and evaluate its worth. This evaluation may take the form of the judgement of a single editor or editors, or a full peer review process.
Public validation of subsequently approved texts may take several forms. At its most formal, the editor may republish the article with explicit approval. Approval might take the form of an addition to the text or its metadata. Or the editor may simply link to the article, via the table of contents of the overlay journal. An alternative approach is to link to articles already published in various open access ejournals, but adding value by grouping scattered articles together as a single themed issue of the overlay journal. Such themed issues allow the focussed coverage of relatively obscure or newly emerging topics.
http://en.wikipedia.org/wiki/Overlay_journal

—*Published contribution to a discussion in a journal (Pre-print/post-print)*

ANTHOLOGY

An anthology is a collection of literary works chosen by the compiler. It may be a collection of poems, short stories, plays, songs, or excerpts. In genre fiction anthology is used to categorize collections of shorter works such as short stories and short novels, usually collected into a single volume for publication. The complete collections of works are often called Complete Works or Opera Omnia (Latin language equivalent). http://en.wikipedia.org/wiki/Anthology

CONFERENCE POSTER

The Conference Poster is a central part of a Poster Session or Poster Presentation which is common at scientific congresses or conferences. During a poster session researchers accompany a paper poster (Conference Poster), illustrating their research methods and outcomes. The poster itself varies in size according to conference guidelines from 2x3 feet to 4x8 feet in dimensions (approximately 60x90cm to 120x243cm). Posters are often created using a presentation program such as PowerPoint and may be printed on a large format printer. Posters are often laminated with plastic to improve durability. http://en.wikipedia.org/wiki/Poster_session (+ changes)

CONFERENCE PROCEEDINGS

In academia, proceedings are the collection of academic papers published in the context of an academic conference. They are usually distributed as printed volumes or in electronic form either before the conference opens or after it has closed. Proceedings contain the contributions made by researchers at the conference. They are the written record of the work that is presented to fellow researchers. http://en.wikipedia.org/wiki/Conference_proceedings

Publication Taxonomy Extendend

COURSE READER
A course reader is a publication type used for teaching in universities and academe. A course reader is made up of a collection of existing texts, course slides and notes etc. Common forms of course readers include; photocopy packs or PDF documents.
https://en.wikipedia.org/wiki/Course_reader

EDITED BOOK, EDITED COLLECTION, FESTSCHRIFT (GERMAN), PUBLISHED READER
An edited book features articles or other material on the same subject but by different authors collected together in one book by an editor.
http://www.cod.edu/people/faculty/pruter/research/editedbook.htm

EDUCATIONAL PACK
Similar to course reader, an accompanying package to the course, including activities, instructions, challenges, discussion themes, visual material to provide concrete interventions for the course to work with the material thought.

ESSAY
An essay is generally a short piece of writing written from an author's personal point of view, but the definition is vague, overlapping with those of an article and a short story.
http://en.wikipedia.org/wiki/Essay

GRADUATE THESIS
a document submitted in support of candidature for an academic degree or professional qualification presenting the author's research and findings.
http://en.wikipedia.org/wiki/Thesis

GREY LITERATURE
Informally published written material (such as reports) that may be difficult to trace via conventional channels such as published journals and monographs because it is not published commercially or is not widely accessible. It may nonetheless be an important source of information for researchers, because it tends to be original and recent. Examples of grey literature include patents, technical reports from government agencies or scientific research groups, working papers from research groups or committees, white papers, and preprints. The term "grey literature" is used in library and information science.
http://en.wikipedia.org/wiki/Grey_literature

MINOR OR REGIONAL LANGUAGE PUBLICATIONS

MONOGRAPH
A detailed written study of a single specialized subject or an aspect of it, usually by a single author.
http://en.wikipedia.org/wiki/Monograph

NON-WESTERN TYPOGRAPHIC BOOK, CHINESE, ARABIC, ETC.

PUBLISHED INTERVIEWS
Appears in various forms and media. You need to request permission from the interviewee. In aural archiving tradition the interview has to be made available for further use to both, the one who conducted the interview and the one you gave the interview.

PUBLISHED READER

PHD THESIS
A dissertation or thesis is a document submitted in support of candidature for a degree or professional qualification presenting the author's research and findings. http://en.wikipedia.org/wiki/PhD_thesis

READING GROUP

READING LIST
Comprehensive list of reading material including reference to supplementary information and alternative perspectives (including audiovisual materials, links, additional, extracurricular readings, etc.)

REFERENCE WORK
A reference work is a book or serial publication to which one can refer for confirmed facts. The information is intended to be found quickly when needed. Reference works are usually referred to for particular pieces of information, rather than read beginning to end. The writing style used in these works is informative; the authors avoid use of the first person, and emphasize facts. Many reference works are compiled by a team of contributors whose work is coordinated by one or more editors rather than by an individual author. Indexes are commonly provided in many types of reference work. Updated editions are usually published as needed, in some cases annually. Reference works include dictionaries, thesauruses, encyclopedias, almanacs, bibliographies, and catalogs. Many reference works are available in electronic form and can be obtained as software packages or online through the Internet. http://en.wikipedia.org/wiki/Reference_work

—Encyclopedia (meta, "all human knowledge")
A type of reference work – a compendium holding a summary of information from either all branches of knowledge or a particular branch of knowledge. Encyclopedias are divided into articles or entries, which are usually accessed alphabetically by article name. Encyclopedia entries are longer and more detailed than those in most dictionaries. Generally speaking, unlike dictionary entries, which focus on linguistic information about words, encyclopedia articles focus on factual information to cover the thing or concept for which the article name stands.
http://en.wikipedia.org/wiki/Encyclopedia

—Compendium
A concise, yet comprehensive compilation of a body of knowledge. A compendium may summarize a larger work. In most cases the body of knowledge will concern some delimited field of human interest or endeavour, while a "universal" encyclopedia can be referred to as a compendium of all human knowledge. It could also be referred to as a tome. The word compendium arrives from the Latin word "compenso", meaning "to weigh together or balance". The 21st century has seen the rise of democratized, online compendia in various fields.
http://en.wikipedia.org/wiki/Compendium

—Handbook (more hands on, instructions, guideline)
A handbook is a type of reference work, or other collection of instructions, that is intended to provide ready reference. A handbook is a treatise on a special subject. Nowadays it is often a simple but all-embracing treatment, containing concise information and being small enough to be held in

the hand. A handbook is sometimes referred to as a vade mecum (Latin, "go with me") or pocket reference that is intended to be carried at all times. It may also be referred to as an enchiridion. Handbooks may deal with any topic, and are generally compendiums of information in a particular field or about a particular technique. They are designed to be easily consulted and provide quick answers in a certain area. For example, the MLA Handbook for Writers of Research Papers is a reference for how to cite works in MLA style, among other things.
http://en.wikipedia.org/wiki/Handbook

—*Manual*
A book of instructions, esp. for operating a machine or learning a subject; a handbook

REPORT
Any informational work (usually of writing, speech, television, or film) made with the specific intention of relaying information or recounting certain events in a widely presentable form.
Written reports are documents which present focused, salient content to a specific audience. Reports are often used to display the result of an experiment, investigation, or inquiry. The audience may be public or private, an individual or the public in general. Reports are used in government, business, education, science, and other fields.
Reports use features such as graphics, images, voice, or specialized vocabulary in order to persuade that specific audience to undertake an action. One of the most common formats for presenting reports is IMRAD: Introduction, Methods, Results and Discussion. This structure is standard for the genre because it mirrors the traditional publication of

scientific research and summons the ethos and credibility of that discipline. Reports are not required to follow this pattern, and may use alternative patterns like the problem-solution format.

Additional elements often used to persuade readers include: headings to indicate topics, to more complex formats including charts, tables, figures, pictures, tables of contents, abstracts,and nouns summaries, appendices, footnotes, hyperlinks, and references. http://en.wikipedia.org/wiki/Report

RESEARCH PAPER, ACADEMIC OR SCHOLARLY PAPER
A Research Paper is a type of academic writing that needs more theoretical, significant and methodical level of question. http://en.wikipedia.org/wiki/Research_Paper

WORKING PAPER
A preliminary scientific or technical paper. Often, authors will release working papers to share ideas about a topic or to elicit feedback before submitting to a peer reviewed conference or academic journal. Working papers are often the basis for related works, and may in themselves be cited by peer-review papers.
http://en.wikipedia.org/wiki/Working_paper

Publication Taxonomy Extendend

Part 2
Unconventional Publications (Academic and Non-Academic), Hybrid and Experimental (Blue Sky)

APPS
An app is a piece of software. It can run on the Internet, on your computer, or on your
phone or other electronic device.
http://google.about.com/od/a/g/apps_def.htmArchive, Collection

ARTIST'S BOOK

BIBLIOGRAPHY
1) a list of books, magazines, articles, etc., about a particular subject; a list of the books, magazines, articles, etc., that are mentioned in a text. http://www.merriam-webster.com/dictionary/bibliography

2) Bibliography (from Greek literally "book writing"), as a discipline, is traditionally the academic study of books as physical, cultural objects; in this sense, it is also known as bibliology (from Greek -logia). Carter and Barker (2010) describe bibliography as a twofold scholarly discipline—the organized listing of books (enumerative bibliography) and the systematic, description of books as physical objects (descriptive bibliography). http://en.wikipedia.org/wiki/Bibliography

BLOG
A blog (a truncation of the expression web log)[1] is a discussion or informational site published on the World Wide Web and consisting of discrete entries ("posts") typically displayed in

reverse chronological order (the most recent post appears first). Until 2009 blogs were usually the work of a single individual, occasionally of a small group, and often covered a single subject. More recently "multi-author blogs" (MABs) have developed, with posts written by large numbers of authors and professionally edited. MABs from newspapers, other media outlets, universities,think tanks, advocacy groups and similar institutions account for an increasing quantity of blog traffic. The rise of Twitter and other "microblogging" systems helps integrate MABs and single-author blogs into societal newstreams. Blog can also be used as a verb, meaning to maintain or add content to a blog.
http://en.wikipedia.org/wiki/Blog

BOOK REVIEW (NON-ACADEMIC)
A book review is a form of literary criticism in which a book is analyzed based on content, style, and merit. A book review can be a primary source opinion piece, summary review or scholarly review. Books can be reviewed for printed periodicals, magazines and newspapers, as school work, or for book web sites on the internet. A book review's length may vary from a single paragraph to a substantial essay. Such a review may evaluate the book on the basis of personal taste. Reviewers may use the occasion of a book review for a display of learning or to promulgate their own ideas on the topic of a fiction or non-fiction work. http://en.wikipedia.org/wiki/Book_review

CATALOG

CHAT STREAMS

CONFERENCE PROCEEDINGS (MULTI MEDIA)

Publication Taxonomy Extendend

COOKBOOK

DISCUSSION FORUMS

E-BOOK

EMAIL

EXHIBITION ZINE

GRAPHIC (NOVEL-TYPE) BOOK

GUIDED TOUR

JOURNAL, SCIENCE MAGAZINE, MAGAZINE (ACADEMIC AND NON-ACADEMIC)
Usually one main theme per issue, regular editorials. Articles chosen and strongly edited by an editing staff (continuous level of quality). Articles are usually accompanied with non-text material such as images series and visualizations. Articles often upon commission or call.

LECTURE

LECTURE VIDEO

LIQUID BOOK

MAP / GEOSPATIAL REPRESENTATION

MEDIUM-LENGTH BOOKS ALONG THE LINES OF AMAZON'S KINDLE SINGLES

MULTI-MEDIA BOOK

NANOPUBLISHING
Blog-based publishing intended for a certain audience
http://en.wiktionary.org/wiki/nanopublishing

NEWSPAPER ARTICLE

NON-CONVENTIONAL JOURNAL

NOTEBOOK (LIKE WALTER BENJAMIN'S)

OBJECTS (DIGITAL/ANALOGUE)

OPEN NOTEBOOK

PAMPHLET
1) A small booklet or leaflet containing information about a single
subject.
https://www.google.de/search?q=define+pamphlet&oq=define+pamphlet&aqs=chrome..69i57j0l5.3410j0j7&sourceid=chrome&espv=210&es_sm=91&ie=UTF-8

2) A pamphlet is an unbound booklet (that is, without a hard cover or binding). It may consist of a single sheet of paper that is printed on both sides and folded in half, in thirds, or in fourths (called a leaflet), or it may consist of a few pages that are folded in half and saddle stapled at the crease to make a simple book.
In order to count as a pamphlet, UNESCO requires a publication (other than a periodical) to have "at least 5 but not more than 48 pages exclusive of the cover pages"; a longer item is a book.
http://en.wikipedia.org/wiki/Pamphlet

Publication Taxonomy Extendend

PODCASTS

RAPID SMS
RapidSMS is a toolset for rapidly building SMS (text message) services for data collection, streamlining complex workflows, and group coordination using basic mobile phones — and can present information on the internet as soon as it is received. So far RapidSMS has been customized and deployed with diverse functionality: remote health diagnostics, nutrition surveillance, supply chain tracking, registering children in public health campaigns, and community discussion.
RapidSMS was designed to be customized for the challenges of governments, multilateral, international- and non-government organizations, and development practitioners: working effectively in spite of geographical remoteness of constituents, limited infrastructure (roads, electricity), and slow data collection (due to paper-based records, slow courier systems, etc). https://www.rapidsms.org/about/

RSS FEEDS
RSS (Rich Site Summary); originally RDF Site Summary; often dubbed Really Simple Syndication, uses a family of standard web feed formats to publish frequently updated information: blog entries, news headlines, audio, video. An RSS document (called "feed", "web feed", or "channel") includes full or summarized text, and metadata, like publishing date and author's name. RSS feeds enable publishers to syndicate data automatically. A standard XML file format ensures compatibility with many different machines/programs. RSS feeds also benefit users who want to receive timely updates from favourite websites or to aggregate data from many sites.
Once users subscribe to a website RSS removes the need for them to manually check it. Instead, their browser constantly

monitors the site and informs the user of any updates. The browser can also be commanded to automatically download the new data for the user.
http://en.wikipedia.org/wiki/RSS

SMS
Short Message Service (SMS) is a text messaging service component of phone, web, or mobile communication systems. It uses standardized communications protocols to allow fixed line or mobile phone devices to exchange short text messages.
http://en.wikipedia.org/wiki/Short_Message_Service

STORIFY
Storify is a social network service that lets the user create stories or timelines using social media such as Twitter, Facebook and Instagram. Storify was launched in September 2010, and has been open to the public since April 2011.
http://en.wikipedia.org/wiki/Storify

TED BOOKS
Shorter than a novel, but longer than a magazine article -- a TED Book is a great way to feed your craving for ideas anytime. TED Books are short original electronic books produced by TED Conferences. Like the best TED Talks, they're personal and provocative, and designed to spread great ideas.
TED Books are typically under 20,000 words — long enough to unleash a powerful narrative, but short enough to be read in a single sitting. http://www.ted.com/pages/tedbooks

TEXTBOOK
A textbook or coursebook is a manual of instruction in any branch of study. Textbooks are produced according to the demands of educational institutions. Although most textbooks

are only published in printed format, many are now available as online electronic books.
http://en.wikipedia.org/wiki/Textbook

THE ATAVIST AND STANFORD LITERARY LAB PAMPHLETS

TWITTER
Twitter is an online social networking and microblogging service that enables users to send and read "tweets", which are text messages limited to 140 characters. Registered users can read and post tweets, but unregistered users can only read them. Users access Twitter through the website interface, SMS, or mobile device app. http://en.wikipedia.org/wiki/Twitter

TRANSMEDIA - DISTRIBUTED STORYTELLING

VIDEO DOCUMENTATION

VIDEO ESSAY
a video which presents factual information about a specific topic.

WHITE PAPER
A white paper is an authoritative report or guide helping readers to understand an issue, solve a problem, or make a decision. White papers are used in two main spheres: government and business-to-business marketing.
http://en.wikipedia.org/wiki/White_paper

WIKIS

ZINE
Most commonly a small circulation of self-published work with original and/or appropriated texts and images.
http://en.wikipedia.org/wiki/Zine

VISUAL APPENDIX

AN IMAGE GALLERY OF PUBLICATION EXAMPLES

Visual Appendix

RAPID WRITING, RAPID PUBLISHING
pads, software, physical space, event, velocity, volume, hardcopy book as proof of existence/work

"As new technologies come into play, people become less and less convinced of the importance of self expression. Teamwork succeeds private effort."

—Marshall McLuhan

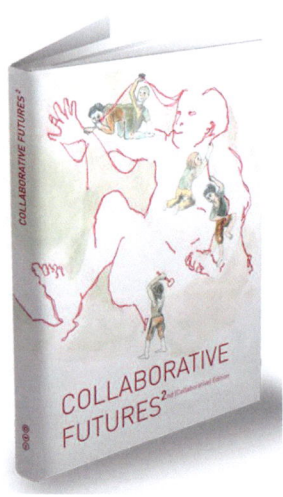

PSYCHOECONOMY
Write a declaration in two days on a joined pad and publish it in a brochure
http://www.psychoeconomy.org/

COLLABORATIVE FUTURES
The future of collaboration, written collaboratively. A book sprint.
http://collaborative-futures.org/
http://booki.cc/ CollaborativeFutures/

A Publication Taxonomy

THE MAGOT
Collective novel from Brendan Howell's exquisite_code project. The book was written by seven writers. The process delegated by a brutalist-brut software edit machine, known as The Maggot.

A software worm that ruthlessly delegates and mediates the work of a group of writers, simultaneously composing a collective text.
http://www.mediascot.org/

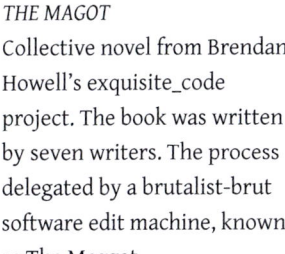

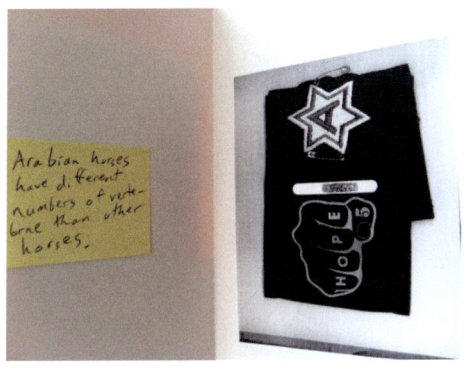

POP UP LIBRARY
temporarily installed library and knowledge generator inside a library's elevator engaging its visitors.
http://cargocollective.com/ fabagit/Pop-Up-Library

Visual Appendix

DIGITAL PUBLICATIONS

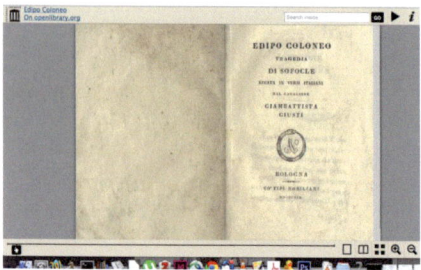

OPEN LIBRARY
digital public library maintain by Archive.org
https://openlibrary.org/

SCALAR
Rich-media online publications
Example publication, Filmic Texts and the Rise of the Fifth Estate, Virginia Kuhn
http://scalar.usc.edu/showcase/ filmic-texts-and-the-rise-of-the- fifth-estate/

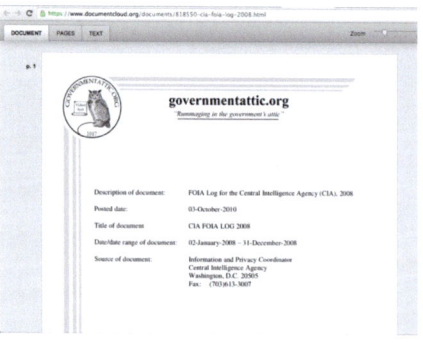

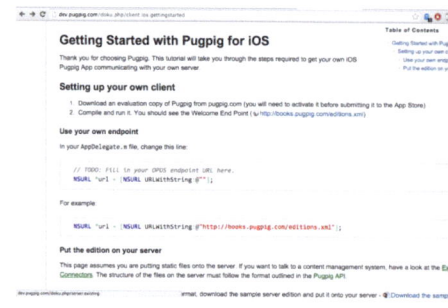

DOCUMENT CLOUD
document analytics, documents as data
http://www.documentcloud.org/

PUGPIG
open source framework for tablet and mobile publications. Example putblication: Time Higher Education Magazine - tablet app. *http://pugpig.com/#the*

A Publication Taxonomy

SOCIALBOOK
social reading, software by
Bob Stein of The Institute for
the Future of the Book
http://livemargin.com/

"To take on a materialist
stance [...] is to acknowledge
that the consequentiality of
objects in the social world
in some way goes beyond
what human intentions
invest in them. Often it is
a general durability and
visibility of things (as
opposed to ephemeral
human interactions) that are
seen a contributing
to the making of society."
—Jenna Burrell

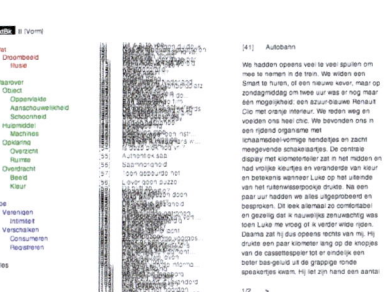

TXTBK BY JOOST BOTTEMA
a book written on a website,
over time.
http://www.robott.org/book2/

35

Visual Appendix

CARDS, ZETTEL, ANSWERS, COMPOSITIONS SERENDIPITOUS READING & ALGORITHM

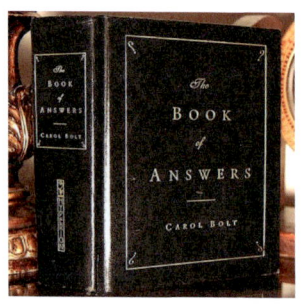

THE BOOK OF ANSWERS
First as thick book and now as website or app with algorithm
http://www.thebookofanswers. com/original_ans.html

OBLIQUE/OPAQUE STRATEGIES
by Brian Eno and Peter Schmidt
It used to be sold as a box of cards (unbound), now it is located on a website. It was originally created and continuously revised between 1975-1979.

The semi instructive nature of this project allows for tiny components. The algorithm provides serendipity.
http://www.opaquestrategies. com/

COMPOSITION NO. 1
by Marc Saporta's was first conceived in 1961, and re-born digitally (~2011) as an iPad app by Visual Editions

A Publication Taxonomy

COMPREHENSIVE PUBLISHING, EVENTS, EXHIBITIONS, SOUNDS, SITES

NOVEL ~ S.C

TEMPORARY SITE
a print magazine, an exhibition, events and a website per publication with resources from the archives and moving images and sound bites
http://temporarysite.org/

VISUAL EDITIONS
event to promote and work with the published sheets of composition No. 1
http://www.visual-editions.com/

Visual Appendix

CELL PHONE PUBLISHING

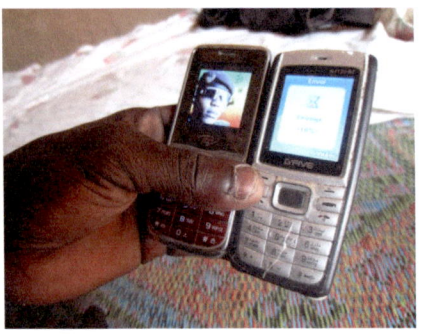

SAHEL MUSIC
Cell Phone file sharing
http://hereandnow.wbur.org/2013/02/25/mali-cellphone-music

TVShows
Displays a list of TV shows which have ✉ shows
new episodes airing today.
by *Hassan Shamim*

Quotify
Adds quotes to random words and ✉ quotify
phrases within the input text.
by *Joel Terry*

Haiku
Get a random haiku, powered by ✉ haiku
isitahaiku.com
⏴ haiku (42458)
by *Cory Forsyth*

THE DUMB STORE
apps for feature phones
http://www.dumbsto.re/

A Publication Taxonomy

SMALL PUBLICATIONS

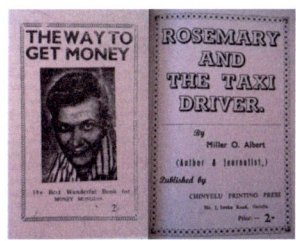

BETTA
A two page zine, a foldable poster
http://cargocollective.com/cityaslab/Betta

ONITSHA MARKET LITERATURE
A pamphlet series from the 50s and 60s published in the Onitsha market in Nigeria—pulp fiction and didactic handbooks
http://onitsha.diglib.ku.edu/index.htm

100 NOTES 100 THOUGHTS
a pamphlet series in three Din sizes in accordance to the amount that is being published
http://d13.documenta.de/#/publications/100-notes-100-thoughts/

Visual Appendix

EDUCATION PACK

TATE MODERN'S EDUCATOR NOTES
In Gallery and online resources
http://www.tate.org.uk/learn/teachers

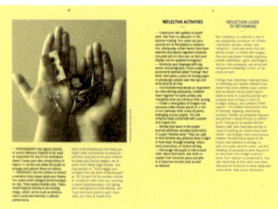

CROWDSOURCING CREATIVITY

NEARLYOLOGY
tell us your nearly stories on a variety of platforms (and events). An initiative by if:book UK
http://www.ifbook.co.uk/

LEARNING TO LOVE YOU MORE
crowdsourced art project on the world wide web. Participants accepted and adhered to an assignment, completed it by following the simple but specific instructions, sent in the required report (photograph, text, video, etc.), and saw their work posted on-line.
http://www.learningtoloveyoumore.com/

SIGNIFICANT OBJECT
extraordinary stories about ordinary things
http://significantobjects.com/

Visual Appendix

POLITICAL ENGAGEMENT, COMMENTS

THE IRAQ REPORT
Lapham's Quarterly in association with The Institute for the Future of the Book. Individuals were invited to annotate the ISG report as well as the President's January speech to the nation. Including such remarks as revisions, clarifications, corrections, translations into plain English.
http://www.futureofthebook.org/iraqreport/

(SEMI) AUTOMATED STORYTELLING THINGS THAT WORK WELL ON TWITTER & OTHER REALLY SHORT PUBLICATIONS

THE LONGEST POEM
A continuous stream of real-time tweets that rhyme.
http://www.longestpoemintheworld.com/

A Publication Taxonomy

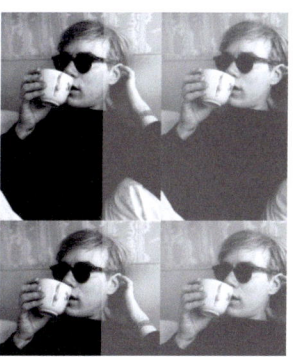

STORIFY
"Collecting updates from social networks [...] to create a new story format that is interactive, dynamic and social."
https://storify.com/

TWITTER
An online social networking and microblogging service that enables users to send and read "tweets", which are text messages limited to 140 characters. Some voices seem predestined for twitter.
http://en.wikipedia.org/wiki/Twitter

SKYWRITE
"Common personal skywriting messages are:
- I Heart U
- I Love U
- Happy B Day
- Marry Me
- I'm Sorry"

http://www.skywrite.com/index.php

Visual Appendix

NEO (E)MAIL ART

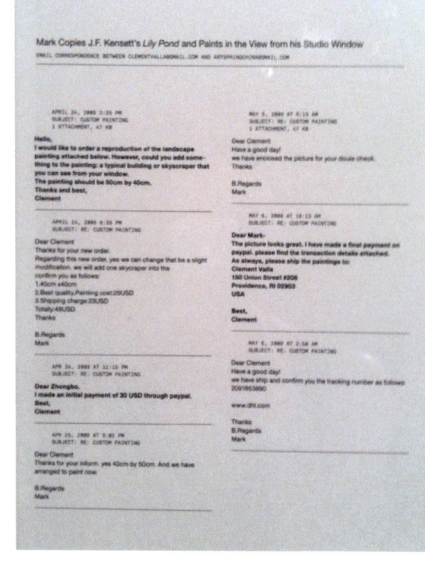

BETWEEN ARTISTS
Published Artist to artist email conversations.
http://www.artresourcestransfer.org/

VANISHING POINT
Comissioned oilpainting China/New York negotiated via an email exchanged.
http://www.bitforms.com/vanishing-point/clement-valla-zhongbo-adds-a-skyscraper-to-j-f-kensetts-almys-pond-newport

A Publication Taxonomy

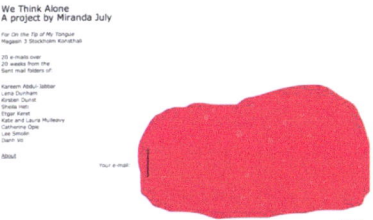

WE THINK ALONE BY MIRANDA JULY
Email art work. (Famous) correspondance were asked to share from their email archive according to certain instructions.
http://wethinkalone.com/

Visual Appendix

BOOK ART
ART BOOK

GEORGE ADEAGBO
Book altars, multiple entry points and books and other objects

THREE STAR BOOKS
"The term "book" is interpreted loosely, as the final product often exceeds the physical and conceptual parameters of publishing. Editions have included aluminum sculpture, wooden reliefs, glitter paintings, and other outgrowths of a given publication."
http://www.threestarbooks.com/

MODULAR CUISINE

THE FAMILY MEAL
a cookbook as a concept for modular and interchangable publishing by El Bulli

Visual Appendix

"Objects themselves are "effects of stable arrays or networks of relations" (Law 2002, 91) This means that rather than look for an object's immanent material properties [...] one looks for how this materiality is distinctively expressed in the way an object comes to be situated in unfolding actions. An object may thus be made material by what surrounds and engages it. In particular, it may be materialized by users (and other actors) who define novel ways of relating it to the other entities in their life world. [...] treating objects and specifically technologies as materially consequential but flexibly and nondeterministically."
—Jenna Burrell,

Printed by Libri Plureos GmbH in Hamburg, Germany